Dec. 2012

with lots of love
from Helga and Jürgen

South Africa

THROUGH THE SEASONS

South Africa

THROUGH THE SEASONS

DENISE SLABBERT

STRUIK
TRAVEL &
HERITAGE

Contents

WINTER *78*   SPRING *116*

Fact File

Total area	1 219 086 km² (about five times the size of the United Kingdom, three times the size of Germany and twice the size of France)
Coastline	3 573 km (including all indentations) 2 997 km (on a smoother line)
Oceans	Atlantic Ocean (west), Indian Ocean (east)
Average annual rainfall	464 mm
Lowest recorded temperature	–18.6 °C at Molteno, Eastern Cape, June 1996
Highest recorded temperature	50 °C at Dunbrody, Sundays River Valley, Eastern Cape, November 1918
National parks	19 (covering about 6% of South Africa)
Total population	48.6 million
Country capitals	Pretoria: Capital of South Africa, administrative capital Cape Town: Legislative capital, home to parliament Bloemfontein: Judicial capital, home to the Supreme Court of Appeal

Provinces and capital cities		
Eastern Cape	Bhisho
Free State	Bloemfontein
Gauteng	Johannesburg
KwaZulu-Natal	Pietermaritzburg
Limpopo	Polokwane
Mpumulanga	Nelspruit
Northern Cape	Kimberley
North West Province	Mafikeng
Western Cape	Cape Town

Official languages	11: Afrikaans, English, Ndebele, Northern Sotho, Sotho, Swati, Tsonga, Tswana, Venda, Xhosa, Zulu
Neighbours	Namibia, Botswana, Zimbabwe, Mozambique
Internal kingdoms	Swaziland, Lesotho

Sources: South African Weather Service; Chief Directorate: Surveys and Mapping; South African National Parks; Statistics South Africa

ZIMBABWE

Mapungubwe National Park

Musina
SOUTPANSBERG

Louis Trichardt (Makhado)

LIMPOPO

Polokwane

Haenertsburg

Kruger National Park

Marakele National Park

Madikwe Game Reserve

WATERBERG

BOTSWANA

Pilanesberg National Park

Mashishing

Nelspruit

MAGALIESBERG

Pretoria

MPUMALANGA

Mmabatho

Mafikeng

Soweto

Johannesburg

GAUTENG

Mbabane

**M
O
Z
A
M
B
I
Q
U
E**

Maputo

NORTH WEST PROVINCE

Kgalagadi Transfrontier Park

Potchefstroom

SWAZILAND

Ndumo Game Reserve

Kosi Bay

Sodwana Bay

Molopo

Vaal

Welkom

Golden Gate Highlands National Park

Hluhluwe-iMfolozi Park

iSimangaliso Wetland Park

Upington

KWAZULU-NATAL

Kimberley

FREE STATE

Clarens

Royal Natal National Park

Nottingham Road

Mokala National Park

Bloemfontein

Maseru

LESOTHO

uKhablamba-Drakensberg Park

Pietermaritzburg

Durban

Orange

NORTHERN CAPE

DRAKENSBERG

Rhodes

SOUTH AFRICA

Great Karoo

EASTERN CAPE

Mountain Zebra National Park

Great Kei

Camdeboo National Park

Bhisho

N

Karoo National Park

Beaufort West

Graaff-Reinet

Sundays

Addo Elephant National Park

East London

0   100   200   300 km

WESTERN CAPE

udtshoorn

Garden Route National Park

Great Fish

Grahamstown

George

Knysna

Plettenberg Bay

Port Elizabeth

ossel Bay

I n d i a n   O c e a n

Introduction

South Africa boasts some of the most dramatic landscapes in the world. Formidable mountain ranges slope down to a coastal strip that stretches from Maputaland in the far northeast on the border with Mozambique to the mountainous Cape at the southern tip of the African continent, and north to the mouth of the Orange River, a ribbon of water that flows through the dry northwestern region, separating South Africa from its arid northern neighbour, Namibia.

Ancient indigenous forests dot the southern and southeastern littoral, while the windy, desiccated west supports mostly hardy scrub and miniature succulents. The eastern reaches of the coastline are luxuriant, verdant and subtropical.

Rain, hail, fog, snow, moonlight and sunshine pass over this land, playing with contrasts, hues and shadows, accentuating textures and experimenting with an endless palette of colours. In this book, the work of some of South Africa's finest nature and travel photographers conveys a hint of the yearlong magic show that unfolds as the country is transformed, time and again, by the passing of the seasons.

Two major ocean currents influence weather patterns not only along the coast, but far inland.

The majestic Drakensberg Amphitheatre in the Royal Natal National Park, with the Tugela River running by, is lush and green in summer, yet dry and snowcapped in winter with lovely clear blue skies.

The cold Benguela current flows north from the Antarctic along the west coast. Its icy, nutrient-rich water has an immediate consequence for the region – the sea is cold, even in summer, but it teems with life and sustains a flourishing fishing industry. The Agulhas current travels south along South Africa's east coast, introducing warm water from the equatorial reaches of the Indian Ocean. Fish is abundant here, too, with the added attraction of coral reefs. The contrasting nature of these water bodies affects not only the climate, but has also shaped the plant and animal life that inhabits the shores: the west is stark and parched, while the east is lush and green.

Further inland, the most significant topographical feature is the Great Escarpment that covers most of the interior. A majestic natural structure formed by the forces of tectonic uplift and erosion, it is at its most spectacular in the mighty Drakensberg range, where it drops more than 3 000 metres to the gently undulating coastal lowlands.

The country is classified as semi-arid, which means that it is regarded as relatively dry with a high sunshine ratio. Rainfall decreases from east to west and the annual average is under 500 millimetres, but averages are deceiving: in the driest province, the Northern Cape, precipitation is scant, while the annual mean for KwaZulu-Natal, Gauteng and Mpumalanga, on the other hand, is significantly higher than the national average. While most of the country gets its rain in summer, the Western Cape is a winter-rainfall region.

If geography dictates the baseline to which the oceans add their perpetual rhythm, then the sun is conductor of the symphony of seasons. As planet Earth orbits the bright star on her annual pilgrimage, she seems to tilt in reverence of the life-giving light. Since South Africa lies in the southern

The Hex River Valley in the Western Cape is vibrant year-round, showing off gorgeous green vines in summer which mature to rich reds, oranges and browns come autumn.

hemisphere, the seasons are inverted, and the end of the year signals that summer is in full swing.

The South African summer, from December to February, is a lively movement – the sun is hot and the tempo fast, and almost everyone is out and about. This is a vibrant time characterised by vigorous outdoor activity: there are joggers, walkers and cyclists on the streets, hikers and rock-climbers in the mountains, and kayakers, surfers and divers in the sea. Camping grounds are full and the tempting smell of the ubiquitous braai (barbecue) mingles with the sweet scent of sun lotion. Summer is the 'can-do' time of the year, and wherever you are in the country people are planning their spare time around the great weather. The academic year has drawn to an end and students take a well-earned break; families gather to celebrate Christmas and the holidays together. But there is no dreaming of a white Christmas here – a hot sun shining from an

unbelievably blue African sky entices everyone out of doors to enjoy life to the full.

Cooling temperatures herald the onset of autumn's largo towards the end of February. Summer festivities wind down and life seems to get a tad sombre, with the heady frivolity of the sunny months being put aside until the next year. As the season progresses, autumn confidently fastens its grip during the months of April and May so that the moderate weather becomes crisper and a sharp tingle is felt in the morning air.

Apart from brief showers in some parts of South Africa, not much rain falls in autumn. Nevertheless, most of the country is transformed – seemingly overnight – when the trees change from multiple shades of green to earthy tones of ochre, orange, russet and red. Autumn sunsets are magnificent, particularly in the Western Cape where the sky can light up with surreal colours, like a gigantic painted

Sabie in Mpumalanga differs vastly throughout the year, evident here in the contrasting opulent ochres and oranges of autumn and vivid greens of its wet summer.

canvas. Autumn is also the perfect time to plan getaways in the bush – days are still sunny and warm and evenings balmy.

The winter months from June to August continue the slow movement – a time of introspection and hibernation for most of the country. Deciduous fruit trees shut down all but their most basic functions and even human activity seems to slow. Social engagements peter out and people spend more time indoors. Highveld winter mornings can be uncomfortably cold with cutting breezes, while the Western Cape gets rained in, often for days on end. That is not to say that there is nothing to do, however. Swollen rivers make for great water adventures towards the end of the season, and much of the interior experiences cloudless days that are perfect for excursions into nature. The Lowveld areas of Mpumalanga and Limpopo enjoy marvellous weather at this time of year, while the diving is fabulous off the KwaZulu-Natal coast, and the northern beaches remain as inviting as ever.

When the days grow longer again and the nights less severe, the spring intermezzo is a time to reawaken from wintry slumber and inactivity. A sense of renewal and anticipation seems to permeate everyone and everything in September. Flowers bloom and the new arrivals in national parks, game and nature reserves around the country begin to take their first faltering steps into the wild. The dry West Coast is resplendent with wildflowers and large swarms of breeding migrant birds begin to arrive from other parts of Africa.

South Africa is unique, whatever the season. Rich in moods, textures, colours and experiences, it abounds with sights, smells and sounds. The large, vibrant country sways in tune with the seasonal rhythms – always exciting, ever beckoning and never dull.

Seasonal changes can affect the entire look and feel of a town, as seen here in a cold, stark Stellenbosch in winter compared to the lighter touch of spring.

Summer

Sunny South Africa is a premier holiday destination. Each province has its special attractions over the summer months, and offers a diversity of landscapes shaped by variations in rain patterns and differing altitudes – from the saturated greens of the northeastern provinces to the golden yellows and tawny browns of the Western and parts of the Northern Cape.

With a coastline spanning more than 3 500 kilometres, from Alexander Bay in the west to Kosi Bay in the east, visitors are spoilt for choice when it comes to beaches, most of which are ideal for a variety of water sports and endless beach fun. As summer reaches its peak, Cape Town's seashore becomes an international playground, packed with visitors from all corners of the globe. Equally popular and definitely not second-best are the beaches and seaside resorts of the Garden Route, the Eastern Cape and KwaZulu-Natal. The Garden Route is lush and green and, apart from its beautiful coast, is also famed for adventure tourism. Further northeast, the Wild Coast is a more rugged, untamed environment, its secluded beaches often shared only with cattle. Washed by the warm tropical waters of the Indian Ocean, the beaches of KwaZulu-Natal are a favourite year-round destination.

In the interior, Mpumalanga's waterfalls are at their most impressive when the summer rains swell the rivers as they, too, gush towards the coast. More tempestuous are the Highveld thunderstorms, a hallmark of the season, with the friction of hot, brooding summer days exploding in a symphony of sound and light: crashing thunder that seems to shake the earth's very foundations is accompanied by dramatic bolts of lightning that electrify laden skies.

PREVIOUS PAGES The colourful huts on St James Beach stand like obedient soldiers saluting the sun, an iconic image of summertime in the Cape when holidaymakers come out to play on the beaches and swim in the refreshing waters of False Bay, warmer than those on the Atlantic Seaboard.

BELOW AND OPPOSITE Clifton – 'South Africa's Saint-Tropez' – nestles in the majestic Peninsula mountain chain that extends from Signal Hill to Cape Point. Blessed with a Mediterranean climate, Cape Town enjoys hot, lazy summer days that stretch into long, warm evenings.

The V&A Waterfront is Cape Town's most visited destination and is especially popular at the end of the year, when visitor figures are at their highest. Against the backdrop of Table Mountain, this working harbour also contains a multitude of shops, restaurants, world-class hotels and live entertainment. Fun activities on offer for the whole family include visiting the marine life at the Two Oceans Aquarium, boat tours around the harbour and to Robben Island and searching for gemstones in the Scratch Patch.

LEFT On a clear summer's day the view from the Table Mountain aerial cableway is unforgettable. The cable car, with its rotating floor, provides 360-degree views of the city, Lion's Head, Camps Bay and Robben Island. Going up in the cable car is weather-dependent, and it is always a good idea for visitors to take along a warm jacket for the early evenings when temperatures begin to cool down considerably on the top of the mountain.

BELOW Robben Island is one of South Africa's most important heritage destinations, and a major highlight on any trip to the Mother City. Many of South Africa's most famous freedom fighters were incarcerated here, including Nelson Mandela, who spent 18 years on the island. One of South Africa's most potent symbols of freedom, the island-museum is situated some 11 kilometres off the coast of Cape Town and was declared a Unesco World Heritage Site in 1999.

OVERLEAF With temperatures at their peak, Clifton's four fashionable beaches offer the ultimate designer playground, attracting sun-seekers in their droves during long summer days. The First, Second, Third and Fourth beaches are separated by giant granite rocks that provide welcome shelter from the southeasterly wind. Locals will tell you that Fourth Beach is great for family fun while First Beach is for the beautifully bronzed fashionistas and designer crowd.

OPPOSITE AND ABOVE Kirstenbosch National Botanical Garden is renowned for its abundance of Cape flora and more than 22 000 species of indigenous plants. A wide variety of the fynbos of the Cape Floral Kingdom, declared a Unesco World Heritage Site in 2004, may be admired here. Magnificently located on the eastern slopes of Table Mountain, it has much on offer to keep visitors occupied. Themed exhibits include the Fragrance, Medicinal, Cycad and Useful Plants gardens. There are numerous walking paths, including a tactile Braille trail, as well as a variety of interesting sculptures and artworks, and restaurants. The Old Mutual Summer Sunset Concerts take place here where picnickers listen to live music on balmy summer evenings.

OVERLEAF Since the first grapevines were planted in the Cape by Jan van Riebeeck in 1655, South Africa has emerged as one of the world's finest wine-producing nations. Certainly the rolling winelands of Stellenbosch are a highlight on any visit to the Western Cape. Founded in 1971, the Stellenbosch Wine Route is the oldest in South Africa, and is famous for its classical Cape Dutch architecture, lyrical scenery and superb wine-tasting safaris. The moderate climate of the area, with temperatures averaging between 15 and 30 degrees Celsius, provides ideal conditions for the cultivars. Summer is a special time for the winemakers as they wait patiently for the grapes to ripen, in anticipation of an excellent harvest ahead.

BELOW During the hot sunny days from November through to January visitors can go strawberry-picking at Mooiberg Farm, famous for its delicious fruit and small population of scarecrows. Situated between Somerset West and Stellenbosch, the farm, surrounded by vineyards and mountains, is a short drive from Cape Town.

RIGHT The Huguenot Monument lies at the top of Lambrecht Road in Franschhoek, the 'French Corner' of the Cape, and the grounds offer a perfect opportunity to enjoy a summer picnic. For those in search of a quaint eatery, this is legendary food and wine country as the village is home to some of the country's best cuisine and there is plenty of good wine to sample. The Cap Classic and Champagne Festival in December attracts visitors in droves, as does the winter Bastille Festival in July.

The majestic Knysna Heads are a natural attraction along the Garden Route, the breathtaking stretch of land running up the southeast coast from Mossel Bay to Humansdorp. The turbulent channel between the Heads is a navigational challenge for fishing and leisure boats, no matter what the season. Knysna has a temperate climate but locals will tell you that you can have four seasons in one day in this magical part of the world.

OPPOSITE The lush coastal forests found along the Garden Route, once heavily exploited for their valuable timber, are a sight to behold during the summer months when the pink keurboom flowers in profusion along forest margins and roadsides and in river valleys. Today, most of the forest land is carefully protected and timber harvesting is strictly managed to ensure sustainability.

ABOVE Summer activities in the Tsitsikamma section of the Garden Route National Park include forest canopy tours, hiking, black-water tubing and boating. Storms River Mouth marks the start of the scenic but challenging five-day Otter Trail, which traverses 42 rugged kilometres over clifftops and through rivers as it winds its way west towards Nature's Valley, where the trail ends. Sightings of whales frolicking in the ocean en route are fairly frequent.

The Addo Elephant National Park is situated northeast of Port Elizabeth, on the Sunshine Coast, in a semi-arid to arid region that has an average rainfall of less than 495 millimetres, with slightly more precipitation along its coastal section. It started off with just 11 elephants in 1931 – and today there are more than 450 of the gentle giants roaming a reserve that now covers some 164 000 hectares. Apart from the expanding elephant population, the park is home to buffalo, rhinoceros, lion and leopard, not to mention southern right whale and great white shark.

LEFT The Eastern Cape's Wild Coast is known for its rugged scenery and pristine coastal landscape. A favourite activity is taking a canoe trip along the Mtentu estuary. Here, abundant forests hug the riverbanks and paddlers can view a large waterfall as they make their way through a forested gorge to inspect a mystical cave, said to be used by local sangomas (traditional healers). Mtentu Camp makes a handy base from which to explore the area. It overlooks the Mkambati Nature Reserve, one of the world's biodiversity hotspots.

OVERLEAF Durban, the principal city of subtropical KwaZulu-Natal, has a yacht basin that provides mooring for many watercraft. Close to the city, with scenic views of buildings and hotels that hug the coastal road, it has some great restaurants and pubs. KwaZulu-Natal is warm all year round, though the summer rains refresh hotter summer temperatures that peak in the low thirties. The sea here averages 21 degrees Celsius.

OPPOSITE Synonymous with summer holidays in Durban is a rickshaw ride. Once called the 'poor man's taxi', rickshaws became fashionable with Durban tourists as far back as the 1920s. Certainly the exotic headdresses and colourful costumes of the rickshaw pullers add to the summer holiday feel of this city, which is affectionately known as 'Durbs-by-the-Sea' in the local patois.

THIS PAGE In summertime, Durban offers a heady mix of fragrances, sights and tastes that suggest long, hot days and nights. The sweet fragrance of frangipani (top left and bottom right) blends with the exotic aroma of spices, and the deep purple of aubergines (top right) offsets the vivid yellow of turmeric (bottom left) – hinting at the promise of a glorious prawn curry served up with views of the ocean.

Ndumo Game Reserve lies on the border with Mozambique and adjacent to Tembe Elephant Game Reserve. The area is known for having the highest bird count of any reserve in South Africa, with more than 420 species. There are also nyala, bushbuck, impala, black and white rhinoceros, hippopotamus and the ever-present crocodile. Vegetation consists of thick bush, savannah and extensive forests. Yellow-barked fever trees often line the beautiful water pans.

BELOW AND RIGHT Breathtaking natural beauty makes Kosi Bay a popular ecotourism destination. The highlight must be turtle-tracking safaris, and controlled guided tours are available. Each year loggerhead turtles crawl laboriously onto the beach to lay their eggs. During January and February the hatchlings break out of their eggs and head back to sea, a first journey that is said to be guided by the moon. Other activities on offer include kayaking, snorkelling and boat trips to visit the fish traps managed by the local Tembe-Tsonga people.

OVERLEAF More than 2 153 plant species grow in the Drakensberg. During the summer season the everlastings are out creating carpets of canary yellow, while rare orchids and irises also make a showing. When the berg winds blow it can get very hot, but generally temperatures are moderate during the daytime. It is a good idea to plan hikes for the mornings as the Drakensberg region is renowned for its theatrical thunderstorms in the afternoons. In the evenings, temperatures drop quite considerably.

OPPOSITE The buzzing metropolis of Johannesburg presents its visitors with an added thrill in the summertime when dramatic thunderstorms disrupt the sweltering heat of late afternoons, giving some relief. The rumbling thunder and flashing skies that form a spectacular backdrop to the City of Gold are part of the city's mercurial nature and are over as quickly as they begin.

ABOVE Nelson Mandela Bridge has become a proud icon of Johannesburg, affectionately called Jozi. The bridge lights up at night when party-seekers head from the northern suburbs into Newtown to enjoy the restaurants, pubs and nightclubs on hot, sultry summer evenings. Daytime activities at this time of year include boating on the Vaal Dam, picnicking at Zoo Lake and enjoying the fun park at Gold Reef City.

LEFT The Kruger National Park is where you have a chance to see the Big Five – lion, leopard, rhinoceros, elephant and buffalo – as well as a wealth of other fauna. At almost two million hectares this is South Africa's largest game reserve and a must-see attraction. Accommodation options range from camping to self-catering in a thatch rondavel (traditional round house), or living it up at one of the luxury safari lodges in private concessions located within the park. A visit here offers truly amazing wildlife encounters – you have a choice of game drives or guided walks in the open veld in the company of experienced game rangers. Summer rains go hand in hand with lush vegetation that makes game-spotting a little bit more difficult. This is when you will see more on foot than you would from your vehicle.

BELOW The African jacana is very much at home walking on the lily pads at Lake Panic in the Kruger National Park. These birds breed during the summer months and males of the species, who take care of incubation, are known to be very territorial about their nesting areas.

THIS PAGE After the summer rainfalls the watering holes are full, the bushveld is lush and green and the animals enjoy nature's abundance: a chacma baboon snacks on a few leaves (top left); a cheetah takes a wakeful siesta in the green grass (top right); a steenbok has more than enough vegetarian fare to eat (bottom left); and a hippopotamus emerges from the water covered in water hyacinth (bottom right).

OPPOSITE Summer is a special time in the Sabi Sand Reserve. The rains have brought rich pickings for a female white rhinoceros that in spite of her huge size is a herbivore. These animals are not docile, however, although the white rhinoceros is less aggressive than its black cousin. Most rhinoceros forage for food during the cooler hours and coat their skin in mud to moderate their temperature.

Mpumalanga's Panorama Route includes a number of dramatic scenic stops. The Berlin Falls near Graskop in the north of the province is one of these. The falls are most spectacular during the summer months when the area experiences maximum rainfall. At around 1 400 metres above sea level, the region has a temperate climate, and it is often misty during the summer season.

Autumn

Autumn is one of the best times to take a road trip through South Africa. The hot weather of summer is replaced by milder conditions, and wherever you go rainfall is relatively low. The scenery does an about-turn as leaves change from red to gold and everything looks like it has been dipped in honey.

The days begin to shorten – the mornings are darker and the sun sets earlier and earlier, a sure sign that winter is on the way. And while the days are usually still warm, there is a chill in the evening air.

While autumn's dance of colour and light is evident around the country, some particularly attractive destinations are the town of Clarens in the Free State, where poplar trees ostentatiously don their autumn coats of burnished yellow, and the city of Durban, where the humidity gives way to crisp, tranquil days. In the vineyards of the Western and Northern Cape, it is a busy time for wine farmers and their labourers as they work to harvest the rich bounty of summer. Their efforts are rewarded with new batches of choice table wines and the more immediate riot of colours as the vines turn from green to gold and russet towards the end of autumn.

Autumn is a great time to venture into the bush; game-viewing can be enjoyed in any of the national parks and game reserves around the country. Hiking and outdoor activities are also more inviting when clear skies and cooler air help to shake off the lethargy of late summer.

PREVIOUS PAGES Tawny-gold poplar trees stretch towards the blue autumn skies near the Golden Gate Highlands National Park in the northeastern Free State, providing cool shade to passers-by.

BELOW AND OPPOSITE Autumn is a beautiful time in the Clarens district of the Free State – when the trees dress in different shades of green and gold in a moving salute to the warm autumn sun.

PREVIOUS PAGES The Golden Gate Highlands National Park, situated in the foothills of the Free State's Maluti Mountains, is celebrated for its dramatic ochre outcrops and expansive blue skies. Although the area receives summer rain, during early autumn the gods have been known to throw in the odd spectacular rainbow, casting a bit of magic in this already exquisite landscape.

OPPOSITE AND THIS PAGE The popular and well-used Sea Point promenade has an energy all of its own, no matter what the season. With the intense heat of summer now but a distant memory, locals exercise in the cool, clear mornings. As the light begins to fade earlier and earlier, sunset is spent running off the day or playing with the kids against the backdrop of a painted sky.

PREVIOUS PAGES One of the most picturesque areas in the country during autumn is the Hex River Valley near De Doorns, which is some 150 kilometres from Cape Town. During autumn the vine leaves can be seen to change from pedestrian green to russet, mocha, yellow and burgundy, creating a carpet of rich earthy tones across the valley. De Doorns Wine Estate is known to have the longest harvest season in the world, and during autumn visitors can enjoy grape-picking in the vineyards.

LEFT AND BELOW The Cederberg Wilderness Area is renowned for both its exquisite rock formations and its ancient rock art. Situated 200 kilometres north of Cape Town near the town of Clanwilliam, the wilderness area stretches across 71 000 hectares of rugged, mountainous terrain. The mountains here consist mainly of Table Mountain sandstone and dramatically weathered formations of this rock, such as the Maltese Cross and the Wolfberg Arch, are typical examples of nature's creative hand in this part of the world. Once home to the San and Khoekhoe people, the rock art here is estimated to be between 1 000 and 10 000 years old. There is an abundance of excellent examples and many of the more than 2 500 discovered rock art sites in the Cederberg are easily accessible. The region is arid to semi-arid and is straddled by the Matjies River which creates a transition between the ever-present fynbos and widespread succulent Karoo vegetation.

OPPOSITE In addition to more than 300 zebra, blesbok thrive in the Mountain Zebra National Park in the Eastern Cape Midlands. Kudu, Cape buffalo, eland, gemsbok, black rhinoceros, cheetah and caracal are also at home here.

ABOVE The barren Great Karoo experiences 260 millimetres of rainfall throughout the year, yet a number of small rural towns prosper here. Situated in the horseshoe bend of the Sundays River, at the heart of the merino and wool industry in South Africa, is the once-frontier settlement of Graaff-Reinet, surrounded by the Camdeboo National Park.

OVERLEAF Cape Vidal is situated within the iSimangaliso Wetland Park – South Africa's first World Heritage Site, proclaimed in 1999. The warm Agulhas current is the reason for the clear waters along this coastline that is renowned for its pristine coral reefs, its long, white sandy beaches, its lakes and swamps, and a diverse habitat that attracts a number of unique bird and animal species.

One of the premier diving and snorkelling destinations in Africa, Sodwana Bay is also very popular with anglers. The bay's superb coral reefs support more than 800 species of fish and marine life such as the loggerhead turtle. The best diving takes place from mid-autumn in April to the beginning of spring in early September when visibility is excellent, although Sodwana offers excellent diving opportunities at any time of the year.

LEFT The area surrounding quaint Himeville, near the uKhahlamba-Drakensberg Park World Heritage Site, is particularly spectacular in autumn. The region feautures tranquil lakes and plentiful dams hopping with trout. During these days the trees show off the season's most fashionable colours with wild abandon.

OVERLEAF The Marakele National Park in Limpopo is embraced by the rugged landscape of the Waterberg Mountains. Its location in a transitional zone between the dry region in the west and the more tropical climate in the east creates a unique habitat for diverse animals and plants. Cedar trees, cycads, tree ferns and even the odd yellowwood are found here, as is a wide variety of animals, including the endangered Cape vulture. The temperatures steadily decrease from an early autumn high of 33 to a late autumn low of 13 degrees Celsius.

The spectacular Augrabies Falls were once called *Aukoerebis* by the Khoekhoe people, meaning 'Place of Great Noise', an evocative description of the roaring sound created when the Orange River plummets down the falls in full flood in early autumn. The volume of water eventually carried over the falls depends on the summer precipitation in the country's northeastern provinces, where several tributaries flow into the Orange, as well as the excess water released from dams along its course. At their highest section, named Bridal Veil, the falls impressively plunge down 75 metres, while the main falls are 56 metres high.

Winter

While South Africa is celebrated for its warm weather, visitors are in for a wintry surprise from June onwards. Fewer tourists are around, making this a great time to explore the country. The considerable span of South Africa's climate range is, perhaps, most apparent in winter when regional displays of the season are strongly contrasted. There might be snow on the Drakensberg peaks, but just a few hundred kilometres away young and old are heading off to the beach in celebration of temperatures that hover around the mid-twenties Celsius. The Western Cape settles in for three months of rain and squally conditions, and wet roads are simply part of the experience. In Gauteng, the cities of Johannesburg and Pretoria experience dry, sunny days, but nights are bitingly cold.

Snowcapped mountains are not unusual at this time of year, and there are several places in the Eastern Cape, Western Cape, Free State and KwaZulu-Natal that receive snowfall. With the arrival of snow comes an instant invitation to indulge in snowball fights and to build snowmen, although the more sports-minded take to skiing and ice-climbing. Other favourite team sports at this time of year are rugby and soccer (football); passionate local supporters follow both local and international matches.

For those who are more interested in the animal kingdom, the annual Sardine Run off the coast of KwaZulu-Natal is a major event on the nature lover's calendar. Winter is also when the whales arrive, and there are plenty of excellent places to admire these magnificent creatures.

PREVIOUS PAGES Nottingham Road is occasionally covered in snow during wintertime. One of the attractions in this part of the world is the Midlands Meander, a series of quaint country towns and small villages between Pietermaritzburg and Estcourt, where visitors can admire local arts and crafts, enjoy fine food and indulge in outdoor activities.

BELOW AND OPPOSITE The coastal city of Durban enjoys temperate winters, boasting more than 320 days of sunshine per year. Air temperatures range from 16 to 25 degrees Celsius and seawater temperatures rarely fall below 19. Winter views of Durban harbour are particularly striking when the sun sets earlier, painting the skies in a wealth of oranges.

The annual Sardine Run is known as the 'greatest shoal on earth', as every year millions of silvery sardines migrate from the cool waters of the Atlantic Ocean to the warm waters of the Indian, attracting large numbers of predators such as sharks and dolphins ready to indulge in a feeding frenzy along the KwaZulu-Natal seaboard. This phenomenon usually takes place from the last two weeks of May until the first two weeks of July, but since nobody can predict the actual day of their arrival, spectators just have to wait and see. In an amazing contrast of shadows, aerial photographs (below) show pockets of light surrounding the sharks as the sardines scatter in an attempt to avoid them. Although more prevalent during the Sardine Run, these hunters are no strangers to this section of the coast, so it is good to know that swimmers are protected by shark nets off Durban's popular beaches.

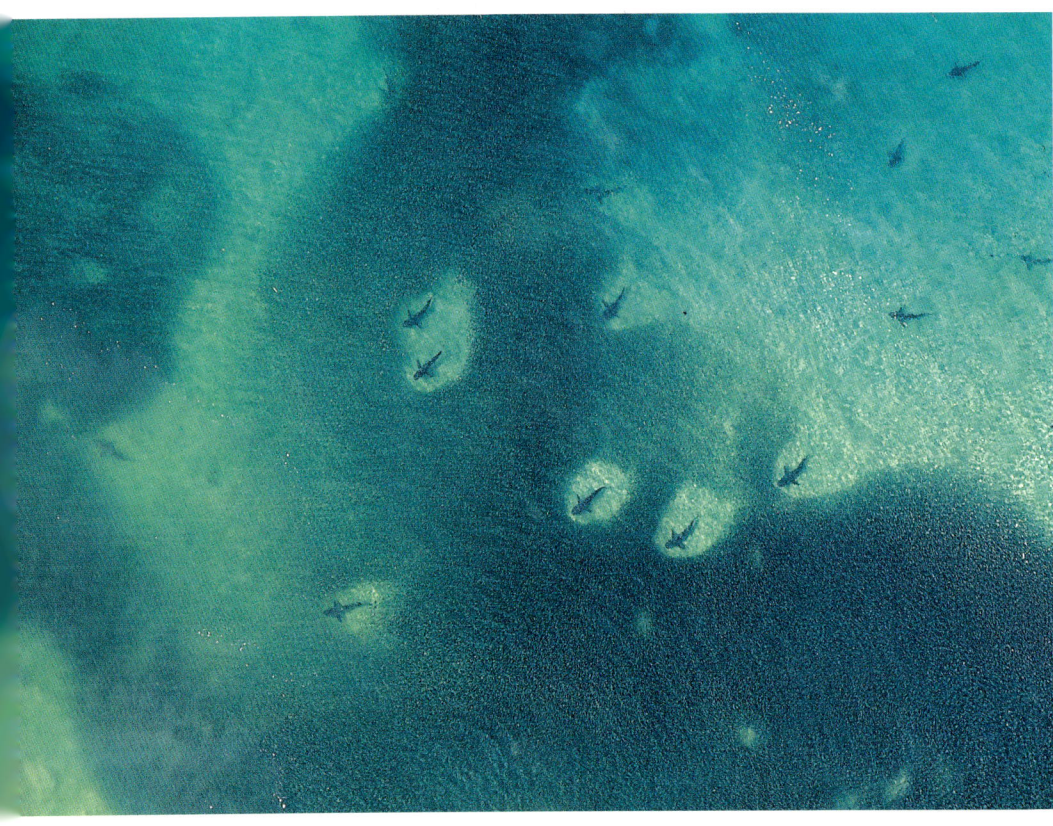

ABOVE The Hluhluwe-iMfolozi Game Reserve lies within the hills and valleys of what was once the realm of mighty Zulu kings. The Hluhluwe section has hilly grasslands, while the iMfolozi portion is more rugged bushveld. Here you will find the colourful mountain aloe. This single-stemmed perennial succulent flowers in winter, daubing an otherwise dry landscape with splashes of robust orange.

OPPOSITE The small town of Himeville, in the foothills of the southern Drakensberg, is renowned for fly-fishing – with more than 60 dams found in the vicinity. The entire Underberg region is very scenic, but the area is particularly beautiful in winter when a soft layer of snow powders the landscape. Winter temperatures are at their coldest during mid-July, when they can drop to zero during the night.

OPPOSITE The formidable Drakensberg Mountains stretch along almost the entire western boundary of KwaZulu-Natal, reaching heights of more than 3 000 metres. Called 'Dragon Mountain' by the Boer trekkers (pioneers) who migrated to the hinterland in the 1830s, the mountain range is also known by its Zulu name *uKhahlamba*, meaning 'Barrier of Spears'

ABOVE A favourite Drakensberg wintertime activity for thrill seekers is ice-climbing, and those in the know head off to the Makaza Icefall where the waterfall freezes over towards the end of winter. It takes a full day of hiking from Giant's Castle to reach and requires camping in sub-zero conditions, so it is not for the faint-hearted.

OPPOSITE Fine frost delicately lines the edges of a cluster of leaves, evidence of a clear and windless winter night during which the temperature dropped enough to allow water vapour to transform into tiny ice crystals that grow near the ground. Frost appears only in certain regions in South Africa, usually at high altitudes such as here in Nigel, a small mining town near Johannesburg. Although frost can kill plants, most indigenous trees and shrubs are hardy and frost-resistant.

ABOVE During mild Highveld winters the exquisite Mozambique bar butterfly may make its appearance as early as July, but is more commonly seen during the warmer months between September and May. The butterflies of the bar species are among the fastest flying of all tailed butterflies. This Mozambique bar butterfly was photographed in late winter in the hills above the Walter Sisulu National Botanical Garden in Roodepoort near Johannesburg.

Ethereal mists rise over Pretoria's Rietvlei Dam during cooler winter months, when water sports at this popular recreational destination come to an abrupt halt. The area is dry and frosty at this time of year, and temperatures are known to drop below zero during the evenings. The Rietvlei Nature Reserve, in which the dam is located, covers some 3 800 hectares of open grassland. The dam supplies the country's capital with 15 per cent of its water.

South Africans are passionate about sport, and winter is rugby and soccer (football) season when the locals don their most outrageous supporter outfits. Soccer fans show their enthusiasm by blowing vuvuzelas (opposite), air horns which are unique to the country and form an essential part of local soccer culture. Most winter weekends are spent watching the matches at home on television, at a pub with a big screen, or better yet, live at one of the country's fine stadiums.

BELOW A lioness stalks her prey in the Kruger National Park. Lions generally hunt as a team, communicating with each other using subtle body language while keeping completely silent. Although they prefer medium- to large-sized mammals, lions are not picky about their meals, and anything from mice to young elephants are considered fair game.

RIGHT African buffalo are gregarious beasts, and can be found roaming in herds of between 400 and 600 in the Kruger National Park. A herd wanders together here, when winter has turned the leaves of the mopane trees shades of red and gold. During these dry days large groups of animals congregate around the waterholes. A spectator may be alerted to the arrival of buffalo by a special call, which the animals use specifically when approaching water.

OVERLEAF As the sun fades over a small dam near Thakadu River Camp in the east of the Madikwe Game Reserve in North West Province, an inky sky echoes with a chorus of night sounds. Insects, frogs, bats and nocturnal creatures serenade the winter in this place that author Herman Charles Bosman once said was so rich in atmosphere, so typically South African.

LEFT The vast 160 000-hectare desert wilderness that is the |Ai–|Ais/Richtersveld Transfrontier Park straddles South Africa's far northwestern border with Namibia. Hilly, desolate and harsh, it is nonetheless a marvel of biodiversity, containing the richest variety of succulent plants on earth. While temperatures regularly soar to 53 degrees Celsius during blistering hot summers, winter can be bitterly cold.

BELOW The indigenous kokerboom, or quiver tree, is found in the Northern Cape, and gets its name from the fact that San hunters used to hollow out the soft branches of these trees to make quivers for their arrows.

OPPOSITE The small town of Sutherland in the Karoo is one of the coldest places in South Africa, with an all-time low of -16 degrees Celsius recorded in 2003. The snowcapped Saltpeterkop, part of an ancient volcano last active some 66 million years ago, can be seen just outside the town.

THIS PAGE Its clear, dark night skies, arid location and high altitude made Sutherland the ideal site for the South African Large Telescope (SALT) (top). Along with snow, the appearance of hoarfrost crystals (above) add a delicate sparkle to crisp mornings in the area.

LEFT AND BELOW The Free State is farming country, and as a primary producer of grains it is no wonder that it has been dubbed 'South Africa's Granary'. Almost two-thirds of the gross agricultural income of the province is generated by field crops, yet farmers also make a tidy sum from their flocks of hardy merino sheep. In addition to the cultivation of grains, landholders also farm with soya, sunflowers, cherries, asparagus, potatoes and flowers.

OVERLEAF Cape Town's iconic Table Mountain fashionably changes her look with the seasons, as seen here in her winter cloud blanket and rainbow jewels.

LEFT Dungeons, which lies in the imposing shadow of Hout Bay's Sentinel Peak, is renowned as one of the world's biggest and best surf spots, albeit briefly each year, sometime between June and August when winter brings huge waves – some topping out at 10 metres – crashing over the reef. Big-wave surfers flock from around the globe to test their mettle against this force of nature.

BELOW Across the mountain from Hout Bay, Kalk Bay on the False Bay coast is occasionally pounded by massive waves during winter and early spring – an occurrence that at times has led to the flooding of the nearby restaurants and the destruction of concrete structures within the small harbour itself. Offshore storm swells, some originating almost 5 000 kilometres away in the Southern Ocean, are responsible for the occurrence of freak waves along this and other parts of the South African coast.

THIS PAGE Despite wet Western Cape winters, a number of flowers blossom at this time. The edible yellow oxalis (top left) is not only pretty but also has medicinal qualities. Equally becoming are some of the winter-growing succulents of the Aizoaceae family, commonly known as ice plants or *vygies* (top right and bottom left). The spicy-smelling cinnamon hessea (bottom right), a highly threatened lowlands plant species, flowers after fire.

OPPOSITE Rural Ceres in the Western Cape lies in one of South Africa's major fruit-growing areas. In winter this fertile area is covered in snow at least once during the season. At the first sign of snowfall, enthusiasts from as far afield as Cape Town don warm jackets and head for the hills for a day of frolicking about in the icy foothills of the mountains around the small town.

Situated between mountain and sea, the scenic Overberg is dominated by fertile farmlands where sheep and wheat thrive in the months of winter and early spring. The hills and valleys turn a lush green after the first rains, and the towns and surrounding areas along the national road that bisects this region offer a wonderful tableau of rolling green fields and towering mountains covered in snow. July, which is usually when snow falls, is one of the coldest months of the year.

The Eastern Cape is a land of many contrasts, and in winter the rural village of Rhodes displays a muted palette of various shades of brown, while whites and grays are evident on the peaks and slopes of the surrounding mountains. The nearby Tiffindell Ski and Alpine Resort is one of the only places where one can snowboard and ski in South Africa – albeit it for a few short weeks come June. The resort, nestled in the peak of Ben Macdhui, is situated at 3 001 metres above sea level.

Whales are a majestic presence in South African waters during the cooler months of winter and spring. The creatures, which spend the summer months feeding in the Southern Ocean, migrate northwards in winter to mate and calve in the warmer waters off the South African coast. Two of the more common breeds are the humpback (left) and the southern right whale. Humpbacks can be seen anywhere along the eastern coast as they make their way to Mozambique, while their southern right cousins stay south, not travelling further than KwaZulu-Natal. While these gentle behemoths can be viewed from boats, South Africa is blessed with a variety of excellent land-based lookouts as well. These include Port Elizabeth in the Eastern Cape, De Hoop Nature Reserve and Hermanus in the southwestern Cape, False Bay in Cape Town, and Saldanha and Doringbaai on the West Coast.

Spring

South Africa seems to burst into life in spring, as if in defiance of the winter slumber. This is a heady time of new beginnings as most of the country waits for the first rains to sweep away the dust and residue of the previous cold months. Everyone is out and about once again – going back to the beaches, cycling, jogging or walking, with many of the more body-conscious South Africans keen to get back into shape before the Christmas season, which is but a few short months away.

After the equinox in September, days begin to lengthen noticeably. Once more tables and colourful umbrellas line the city pavements as restaurants and coffee shops invite patrons to stop by. In every province nature flaunts new signs of growth and the young of many animal species arrive at this time, signalling yet another link in the circle of life.

In Namaqualand the arid desert is transformed into field upon vibrant field of wildflowers, while in the Limpopo towns of Haenertsburg and Agatha the azaleas blossom in exuberant flurries of frivolous pink. In Pretoria and Johannesburg many streets are sheltered by the lilac umbrellas of jacaranda trees in full bloom, and the Free State, too, has its floral display as bright cosmos fringe fields and highways.

In the major fruit-growing provinces of Limpopo, Mpumalanga, Free State, KwaZulu-Natal and the Western Cape, dormant trees awaken from a deep hibernation. Resuscitated by the first warm rays of sunshine, they reward passers-by with views of their lovely pink and white blossoms.

PREVIOUS PAGES As the sun returns after a cold, wet winter in the Western Cape, spring flowers appear in profusion in the fertile Biedouw Valley in the Cederberg Mountains, carpeting the veld with lively, fresh colours.

BELOW AND OPPOSITE Early spring brings perfect tranquillity to Johannesburg's Zoo Lake. Further north, the streets of Pretoria are festooned in a lilac splendour as the city's abundant jacarandas come into bloom.

PREVIOUS PAGES During early spring, the yachts come out on the Hartbeespoort Dam in anticipation of warmer weather and better sailing conditions. The dam, in the North West Province, is surrounded by the scenic Magaliesberg mountain range and is a popular weekend getaway for the city dwellers of Johannesburg and Pretoria.

OPPOSITE Spring is usually the time when new arrivals begin to find their place in the Kruger National Park. Chacma baboons move around in troops, sometimes as large as 200-strong. The females and their young stay close to the dominant male for safety.

ABOVE Lions have no fixed breeding season and cubs can be seen all year round in the Kruger National Park. These little ones face many challenges from an early age, not only starvation but physical threats both from other predators and incoming dominant males who would kill the cubs to secure their own genetic line.

PREVIOUS PAGES Azaleas bedeck a river bank near the sleepy mountain village of Haenertsburg in a flashy show of colour. Ranging in shades from polite pink and hot cerise to a no-nonsense brick-red, these members of the Rhododendron family thrive in moist, cool conditions. The annual Haenertsburg Spring Fair takes place during the last week of September when the azaleas, cherry blossoms and crab apples are at their most abundant.

RIGHT Limpopo is known as South Africa's 'Garden of Eden'. The province produces mangoes, pawpaws, citrus fruit, litchis, tomatoes, macadamia nuts and avocados in abundance thanks to a high rainfall quota of 620 millimetres per annum. Along with the Eastern Cape, Limpopo is also well known for its tea plantations. Although there has been a decline in tea production in the province, there is currently a programme under way to resuscitate the industry.

OPPOSITE The Namaqua National Park, situated about 50 kilometres inland from the coast, is famed for its spring flower display. The park occupies the only arid biodiversity hotspot on earth. Not only does it contain more bulb flora than any other arid region but roughly a third of its estimated 3 500 plant species are unique to the area. The entire Namaqualand region covers almost 5 million hectares, much of it blessed with an annual display of golden-yellow and orange daisies.

ABOVE The Kgalagadi Transfrontier Park came about when Botswana's Gemsbok National Park and South Africa's Kalahari Gemsbok National Park were merged in 2000 to create a 3.8-million-hectare mega-reserve, double the size of the Kruger National Park. On the South African side, the sparse vegetation of the dry Auob riverbed provides ideal game-viewing spots. Visitors can enjoy sightings of giraffe, antelope, meerkat (or suricate, a member of the mongoose family) and the black-maned Kalahari lion.

Dorper sheep are farmed extensively in Namaqualand, as these animals thrive in arid regions. They were originally bred to withstand dry conditions, but are also farmed in extreme cold and wet areas. Hardy and disease-resistant, dorpers are now the second-largest sheep breed in South Africa.

The idyllic West Coast town of Langebaan is situated on the 17-kilometre long Langebaan lagoon that is popular for its water sports, especially kitesurfing. During spring there are regular winds at an average of 20 knots, but on really blustery days one can expect speeds of up to 35 knots. The stronger gusts become more frequent as summer approaches.

OPPOSITE Springbok are mixed feeders, meaning they graze and browse. They occur in the West Coast National Park along with antelope such as kudu, eland and bontebok. The largest concentration of animals is found in the Postberg Reserve section of the park, which is only open to the public during the spring wild flower season.

THIS PAGE The Cape is home to many colourful birds. A lesser double-collared sunbird alights on a yellow pincushion protea (left), a Karoo prinia straddles two stalks near Somerset West (top right), and an alert Cape bulbul perches atop a bush to keep a watchful lookout (bottom right).

OVERLEAF In Somerset West's Helderberg Nature Reserve, a Cape sugarbird rests on an indigenous 'sugarbush', as this protea species is known locally. This bird is endemic to the fynbos biome where it seeks out its staple diet of nectar and, in a truly symbiotic manner, pollinates the flowers it visits.

While the Western Cape is best known for its grape harvests, it is also a prime deciduous fruit-growing area due to a moderate climate and excellent winter rainfalls, and much of the area's bounty is exported. After their winter hibernation, the fruit trees burst into life in spring with a profusion of pink and white blossoms.

OPPOSITE In spring, on the new moon that occurs between mid-October and mid-November, Durban's large Indian community celebrates Diwali, the Festival of Lights, along with Hindus around the world. The five-day celebration commemorates the Lord Rama's return from exile after defeating the demon Ravana, and the lights signify his triumph over darkness. Although inspired by religion, it is a joyful affair on the streets of Durban and everyone is welcome to enjoy the brightly coloured processions, singing, dancing and fireworks that mark the festival.

ABOVE A great time to experience Durban's Golden Mile is at dawn when a rich haze gently enshrouds the high-rise hotels and holiday apartments, the walkers stride up and down the promenade and the surfers promise themselves just a few more waves before heading off to work or school.

Kosi Bay is located in the northeastern corner of KwaZulu-Natal, close to the border with Mozambique. It is not actually a bay at all, but a system of lakes connected by narrow reed channels and fringed by a lush, tropical forest. A striking feature of the waterways are the fish traps made of reed fences that the local Tembe-Tsonga people have been using for more than 500 years. Local customs guarantee sustainability, as each trap is owned and managed by a particular family, and overfishing is strictly forbidden.

Pink and white cosmos blossoms are synonymous with the Free State in springtime. These hardy plants are not indigenous to South Africa, and yet grow anywhere and everywhere, including along the contoured ridges of ploughed agricultural fields and alongside main highways and small country roads.

Plant life in the 11 600-hectare Golden Gate Highlands
National Park is divided between the grasslands and forested
areas. The park contains more than 60 species of grasses and
a wealth of flowers, including the customary pink and white
cosmos. Two rare bird species can be seen here: the rare
bald ibis and the bearded vulture.

First published in 2009 by Struik Travel & Heritage
(an imprint of Random House Struik (Pty) Ltd)
Company Reg. No. 1966/003153/07
80 McKenzie Street, Cape Town, 8001
PO Box 1144, Cape Town, 8000, South Africa

www.randomstruik.co.za

Publisher: Claudia Dos Santos
Managing editor: Roelien Theron
Project co-ordinator and typesetter: Alana Bolligelo
Editor: Leah van Deventer
Concept design: Beverley Dodd
Designer: Catherine Coetzer
Proofreader: Carla Zietsman
Picture researcher: Carmen Hartzenberg

Reproduction by Hirt & Carter Cape (Pty) Ltd
Printed and bound by Tien Wah Press (Pte) Limited, Singapore

ISBN 978 1 77007 436 1

10 9 8 7 6 5 4 3 2 1

While every effort has been made to ensure that the information in this book was correct at the time of going to press, some details might since have changed. The author and publishers accept no responsibility for any consequences, loss, injury, damage or inconvenience sustained by any person using this book.

Front cover and half title page: Lion's Head from Table Mountain in spring; Title page: the Drakensberg in autumn; Back cover (clockwise from top left, summer through spring): Ndumo Game Reserve, KwaZulu-Natal; Clarens district, Free State; Ceres, Western Cape; Pretoria, Gauteng.

Photographic credits
Copyright in photographs remains with the individual photographers and/or their agents as indicated below.

AF = Africa Imagery; AFP = Afripics; ALB = Albert Froneman; CLB = Colour Library; CM = Chris Marais; DP = Dirk Pieters; DPE = Doug Perrine; FM = Fiona McIntosh; FVH = Friedrich von Hörsten; GD = Gerhard Dreyer; GI = Gallo Images; GN = Greg Nicolson; HVH = Hein von Hörsten; IOA = Images of Africa; JC = Jacques Claassen; JDP = Jéan du Plessis; JF = Justin Fox; JJ = Jeremy Jowell; KY = Keith Young; LVH = Lanz von Hörsten; NA = Nick Aldridge; ND = Nigel Dennis; NPL = Nature Picture Library; OM = Owen Middleton; PA = Photo Access; PP = Phil Perry; RDLH = Roger de la Harpe; RH = Rod Haestier; SA = Shaen Adey; SB = Sam Basch; SW = Steve Woodhall; TC = Tony Camacho; WK = Walter Knirr

Front cover: FVH; Back cover top and bottom left: RDLH/AF; Back cover top right: CM; Back cover bottom right: JDP; Pages 8 left: CLB/IOA; 8 right, 9 right, 24 – 25, 26 left, 136 – 137: LVH; 9 left, 52 – 53, 67, 112, 113, 118, 119, 120 – 121, 132: JDP; 10 left, 20 – 21, 30, 36 – 37, 39 bottom right: KY; 10 right, 26 – 27, 29, 31, 34 – 35, 40 – 41, 42 – 43, 44 – 45, 46, 48 – 49, 58 – 59, 66, 68 – 69, 72 – 73, 78 – 79, 81, 84, 85, 109, 110, 111: RDLH/AF; 11 both: JC; Pg 12 – 13, 15, 17 right, 38, 42 left, 80, 87, 138, 139, 140: SA/IOA; 14 left, 126 – 127, 128: WK/IOA; 16 – 17: HVH; 18 – 19, 28 – 29, 60, 61 (all), 70, 74 – 75: JJ; 22, 107: SA; 19, 23, 76 – 77: FVH/IOA; 32 – 33, 49 right, 54 – 55, 62 – 63, 116 – 117, 129, 133 left and top, 134 – 135: FVH; 39 top left and right, bottom left: DK/IOA; 47, 86, 124 – 125: WK; 50 top (both), 94, 98, 122: ND/IOA; 50 bottom left: LVH/IOA; 50 bottom right: TC/IOA; Pg 51: PP/IOA; 56, 57, 103 right: CM; 64 – 65: OM; 65 right, 99, 102 – 103, 131: HVH/IOA; 71: FM/IOA; 82, 114 – 115: RH/IOA; 83: DPE/NPL/PA; 88, 90 – 91: SB/IOA; 89: SW; 92, 93: GI; 95, 142, 143: AFP; 96 – 97, 104 – 105, 106, 123, 140 – 141: JF; 100, 101 (both): NA; 108 (all): GN/IOA; 130: GD/IOA; 133 bottom: ALB/IOA

Over 50 000 unique African images available to purchase from our image bank at www.imagesofafrica.co.za